Cornerstones of Freedom

The Story of
CHILD
LABOR LAWS

By R. Conrad Stein

Illustrated by Keith Neely

CHILDRENS PRESS™
CHICAGO

Library of Congress Cataloging in Publication Data

Stein, R. Conrad.
    The story of child labor laws.

    (Cornerstones of freedom)
    Summary: Traces the history of laws that were passed
during the early twentieth century to end the exploitation of child laborers that had been widespread since
the beginning of the industrial revolution.
    1.   Children—Employment—Law and legislation—
United States—History—Juvenile literature. [1. Children
—Employment—Law and legislation.   2.   Law—History
and criticism.   3.   Industry—History]   I.   Neely, Keith,
1943-   ill.   II. Title.   III. Series.
KF3552.Z9S73   1984   344.73'0131   84-7017
ISBN 0-516-04679-9   347.304131

Early in the 1900s, a reporter for the *Labor Standard* visited a coal mine near St. Clair, Pennsylvania. There he saw a group of young workers called "breaker boys." They sat hunched over a long coal chute picking out stones and pieces of slate from the coal that rushed by them. The reporter wrote:

"In a little room in this big, black shed—a room not twenty feet square—forty boys are picking their lives away. The floor of the room is an inclined plane, and a stream of coal pours constantly in. They work here in this little black hole, all day and every day, trying to keep cool in the summer, trying to keep warm in the winter, picking away among the black coals, bending over till their little spines are curved, not saying a word all the live-long day.

"These little fellows go to work in this cold dreary room at seven o'clock in the morning and work till it is too dark to see any longer. Not three boys in this roomful could read or write. . . . For this they get $1 to $3 a week. They play no games; when their day's work is done they are too tired for that. They know nothing but the difference between slate and coal."

This was only part of the ugly picture of child labor as it existed in the United States near the turn of this century. At the time, many children from poor families were forced to work exhausting hours for miserable wages. They were denied the right to go to school. The playful moments of childhood were stolen from their lives.

Any child under the age of fifteen who worked full time was considered to be a child worker. A few children began their working lives even before they reached the age of five. By the early 1900s, child labor in America was a national disgrace. As a journalist named Harold Faulkner said, "The picture of children kept awake during the long night in a southern mill by having cold water dashed on their faces, or little girls in canning factories working sixteen hours a day while capping forty cans a minute in an effort to keep pace with a never exhausted

machine...of boys imported from orphan asylums
and reformatories to wreck their bodies in the slavery of a glass factory, or of a four-year-old baby
toiling until midnight over artificial flowers in a
New York tenement—these were conditions that
might well shame a civilized people into action."

Certainly many Americans were ashamed of the brutal specter of child labor. "This great nation, in its commercial madness, destroys its babies," wrote social critic John Spargo. But other Americans saw no great harm in child labor. Many of the child workers were recent immigrants from Europe. Some Americans argued that the child immigrants were better off in the factories since they did not speak English and therefore learned little in school. A few businessmen even claimed that factory work was good for a child. Asa G. Candler, one of the founders of the Coca-Cola Company, said, "The most beautiful sight that we see is the child at labor. As early as he may get at labor the more beautiful, the more useful does his life get to be."

Exactly what is child labor? In all societies, and in every period of history, children have worked alongside adults. In farming communities, children weeded fields or tended herds of cattle. In manufacturing villages, children were taught to carve wood, weave cloth, or make bricks. And children everywhere were expected to do chores in the kitchen.

Children pitching in to help their families is not an example of child labor. Child labor is the exploitation of young workers. Factory owners exploited, or took advantage of, child workers because the owners knew that children would work for less pay than adults. Also, many desperately poor parents exploited their own children by making them toil long hours putting together goods such as artificial flower bouquets, which the parents sold to stores. Clothing manufacturers exploited little girls by using their nimble fingers to run fast-moving, dangerous machines.

Today, laws protect children from being exploited as workers. The laws were passed largely due to the efforts of courageous men and women who were outraged by the sufferings of child workers. Most factory and mill owners bitterly opposed the laws. Because of the laws, the abuses of child labor have all but disappeared in modern America.

The large-scale exploitation of child workers began in England with the era historians call the Industrial Revolution. This era dawned when new machines were invented and businessmen discovered that the factory system could produce goods in numbers that were undreamed of before. The Industrial Revolution started during the late 1700s. From Great Britain it spread to Europe and North America.

The mass production of clothing was a major enterprise during the Industrial Revolution. To produce clothing, families used to work at home spinning cotton into thread and weaving the thread into cloth. The cloth would then be made into shirts, pants, and dresses. The process was laborious and the clothes produced were expensive. Then a series of new inventions revolutionized the clothing industry. In the 1760s, Englishman James Hargreaves created a device called the spinning jenny. This machine spun cotton twenty times faster than the old spinning wheels. New machines for weaving cotton threads also were invented.

Gradually, these machines were hooked up to steam-powered motors, and the Industrial Revolution was under way.

Leading the world in clothing production was Great Britain. By 1835, the country had more than 120,000 steam-powered weaving looms. In many ways the Industrial Revolution improved Great Britain's standard of living. Factories and mills triggered the growth of large cities. But most factory workers did not share in the new prosperity. Work in the factories was monotonous, back-breaking, often dangerous, and almost always low-paying.

The children of British factory-working families were ripe for exploitation. Early in the Industrial Revolution, cotton mill owners realized that little girls possessed the flying fingers needed to keep hundreds of cotton threads flowing smoothly through spinning machines. Mine owners discovered

that small boys could squeeze through narrow shafts to dig for coal. And many employers were quick to take advantage of the fact that hungry children would accept half the wages adults expected.

During Great Britain's Industrial Revolution, thousands of girls and boys spent their childhood sealed up in noisy, stale-aired factories or in dark mine shafts. They learned nothing of the world outside the dismal places where they toiled. According to one story, a clergyman visited an English coal mine and asked a twelve-year-old miner if he knew of God. The boy stared at the preacher with a vacant look on his face. "God?" he asked. "God? No, sir. I don't know him. He must work in some other mine."

It was this Industrial Revolution that the Americans imported from the British.

In the United States, the Industrial Revolution began in New England. During the early 1800s, factories producing cotton goods grew in number. As had happened in Great Britain, the owners of the American mills quickly discovered that high profits could be gained by employing child workers. From cotton mills, child labor spread to mines and factories. For thousands of American children, the Industrial Revolution meant a life that bordered on slavery.

The rise of the American factory system was aided by the masses of European immigrants who flocked to this country late in the nineteenth century. Most of these new immigrants were from the poorer southern and eastern sections of Europe. This wave of immigration reached its peak in the forty-year period between 1870 and 1910. In 1870, a census counted 750,000 workers under the age of fifteen employed in American industry. With thousands of immigrants pouring into New York every week, that figure jumped to 1.7 million by 1900.

In American industry, child workers served primarily in textile mills, in mines, in factories, and in home and neighborhood workshops. In each area, horror stories about their working conditions emerged. Some children had to work as long as sixteen hours a day. A few reports told of children being chained to their machines inside the factories.

The textile mills that produced the nation's clothing long symbolized the plight of American child workers. Mill owners preferred to hire girls because they believed their delicate hands would keep fine thread flowing through spinning machines. In the late 1800s, many textile mills moved from New England to the South. A 1906 report stated that at least sixty thousand children—mostly girls—under the age of fourteen worked in the southern textile mills. Many claimed that the number was even higher. A southern minister named Edgar Gardner Murphy saw and photographed "little children of six and seven years who were at work for twelve and thirteen hours a day in Alabama mills. . . . There are hundreds of little girls who do not appear to be more than nine or ten years of age, at work in the mills, by night as well as day."

As a cruel irony, the girls who worked in the mills generally wore nothing but rags. They would have loved to wear the pretty dresses, cloaks, and bonnets

they helped to make. But those goods were bought only by middle-class and well-to-do people. The working girls who kept the mills running earned far too little to be able to afford the fine clothes made in their factories.

Mine owners usually hired young boys as workers. A job often assigned to them was to work as "breaker boys." Writing in 1906, John Spargo described the appalling and dangerous working conditions of the breaker boys at one Pennsylvania coalfield: "The coal is hard, and accidents to the hands such as cut, broken or crushed fingers are common. . . . Sometimes there is a worse accident: a terrified shriek is heard, and a boy is mangled and torn in the machinery, or disappears in the chute to be picked out later smothered and dead."

Many immigrant children were exploited through a network of home or neighborhood industries called the sweating system. Under this system, factories farmed out work for people to perform either in their tenement apartments or in neighborhood basements. The basement establishments came to be called sweatshops because in them women and children toiled at top speed twelve hours a day. The needlework, cigar-making, and light assembly

industries contracted out much of their work to sweat shops. Often an immigrant who had learned the English language worked as the middle man, or sweater, who parceled out the work to sweatshops or to immigrant families and delivered the finished products back to the factory. Much of the work under the sweating system was carried out behind closed doors in slum neighborhoods. Therefore, even the states that had laws protecting child workers found the laws almost impossible to enforce.

The sweating system was powerfully described in a book published in 1890 called *How the Other Half Lives.* The author, Jacob Riis, told of the extent and

the tragedy of the sweatshops and home industries in New York City's immigrant slums: "In the tenement [sweatshops] the child works unchallenged from the day he is old enough to pull a thread. There is no such thing as a dinner hour; men, women, and children eat while they work. . . . Take the Second Avenue Elevated Railroad at Chatham Square and ride up half a mile through the sweaters' district. Every open window of the big tenements gives you a glimpse of one of these shops as the train goes speeding by. Men, women, and children bending over their machines, half naked, morning, noon, or night it makes no difference; the scene is always the same."

How did the children react to the exploitation of the mines, the mills, and the sweatshops? When they first started their working careers, many were excited. They believed that their new jobs meant admission into the adult world. If they were attending school and did not like it, they looked upon their work as freedom from the drudgery of the classroom. But after just a few weeks in an airless factory or sweatshop, their excitement over the working world vanished. They began to live lives of bewilderment and despair. Many social workers around the turn of the century claimed that they saw fifteen-year-old boys and girls who could easily pass for thirty.

How did the parents of child workers feel about sending their children to low-paying, tedious, and often dangerous jobs? Most parents grieved. But poor people have few choices when it comes to earning a living. One of the crimes of the child labor system was that it took jobs away from adults. In southern mill towns, it was often easier for a person under fifteen to get a job than for an adult. Many families paid their rent and bought their groceries on the meager wages brought home by their children. Some immigrant parents thought there was no harm in their children working, because children in their native European villages had always worked. But those parents confused healthy outdoor work such as picking apples in an orchard with the dangerous and stifling job of running a drill press in a factory.

To many Americans, child labor was a dreadful sickness in the nation's life. The sickness could be cured only by the passage of a strong law forbidding employers to hire children for full-time labor. As the United States entered the twentieth century, a campaign was launched to demand a strict national law abolishing child labor.

Even by 1900, when the exploitation of children was most rampant, many states had long-standing laws on their books that were meant to protect child workers. As early as 1836, Massachusetts passed a law prohibiting the employment of children under the age of fifteen unless those children had at least some schooling the previous year. In 1842, Connecticut limited the working period for children to ten hours a day.

But state laws were difficult to enforce. Poor children, eager for jobs, lied about their age. The employers who wanted to hire child workers

deliberately failed to require a young applicant to prove his or her age. Writer Edwin Markham told of an interview he conducted with a little girl on the steps of a textile mill:

" 'How old are you?' was asked of one of the workers.

" 'Fourteen,' she promptly answered.

" 'How long have you been working in the mill?'

" 'Three years and a half.'

" 'How old were you when you began?'

" 'Thirteen.' "

Finally, in the South, only a few states had passed effective child labor laws. And many southern politicians refused even to consider such laws. Their states benefited from the new industries constantly moving in to take advantage of the cheap labor. Between 1890 and 1900, the number of child workers in the South tripled.

To abolish child labor, laws with teeth had to be passed. Those laws had to be uniform and apply equally to every state in the union. Therefore, they had to come from Washington, D.C. Social workers, teachers, writers, labor leaders, and even some conscience-stricken businessmen joined together to insist that Congress pass effective legislation to eliminate child labor. Those people who wanted to change, or reform, the child labor laws formed the National Child Labor Committee in 1904.

One member of the committee was a hard-driving reformer named Jane Addams. Born to wealthy parents, Miss Addams moved to a Chicago immigrant slum and founded a neighborhood center called Hull House. At the time, immigrants made up two thirds of Chicago's population. Sweatshops operated on every slum block. Through newspaper articles and lectures, Miss Addams alerted the country to the shocking conditions endured by the child worker in Chicago: "During one winter, three boys from a Hull House club were injured at one machine in a neighboring factory for want of a safety guard that would have cost but a few dollars to install .... Another little girl of thirteen employed in a laundry at a heavy task beyond her strength, committed suicide, because she had borrowed three dollars from a companion which she could not repay unless she confided the story to her parents and gave up an entire week's wages—but what could the family live upon that week in case she did?"

Other writers brought the horrors of child labor out of the sweatshops and onto the pages of books and newspapers. A poet named Sarah N. Cleghorn sorrowed over the children confined in the factories and mills all day long, deprived of time to play. Meanwhile, the rich and powerful factory owners enjoyed their leisure hours. About this cruel contrast between playing adults and working children, Miss Cleghorn wrote a simple but moving poem:

> The golf links lie so near the mill
> That almost every day
> The laboring children can look out
> And see the men at play.

Labor unions joined the crusade for a child labor law. Their motives were both humanitarian and

JANE ADDAMS

JACOB RIIS

practical. Children working in factories meant that adult union members were without jobs. Finally, a few businessmen hoped to see an effective child labor law passed. They included even some factory owners who employed children. Businessmen were often forced to hire children because their competitors used child workers and could undersell anyone who refused to do so.

Most businessmen, however, remained opposed to the child labor law. Some industries were so dependent on child workers that the owners feared that without them they would have to shut down. As Jane Addams wrote, "The bitterest opposition came from the large glass companies, who were so

SARAH N. CLEGHORN

EDWIN MARKHAM

accustomed to use the labor of children that they were convinced the manufacturing of glass could not be carried on without it."

During the early 1900s, a war of words raged between the reformers and the factory owners. In 1916, when Congress passed the Keating-Owens Act, it appeared that the reformers had won. This act barred from interstate shipment all goods made by child labor. It required factory owners to check the birth certificates of all young job applicants. Factory owners who violated this law could be sent to jail.

All over the country the reformers hailed their victory. But their rejoicing was short-lived. Just two years after its passage, the Keating-Owens Act was declared unconstitutional by the United States Supreme Court. At the time, many members of the Court were sympathetic to big business. One of the reasons they struck down the act was because it denied children the "freedom" to work. However, none of the justices bothered to ask the children if they really wanted the "freedom" to work twelve hours a day in a noisy factory or a dark mine.

Despite the Supreme Court's ruling, the mood of the country was on the side of the reformers. Both political parties wanted a child labor law passed. So did the American Federation of Labor, the Council of Churches, and the American Medical Association. In 1919, Congress passed another law, this time putting a special tax on the profits from goods made entirely or in part by child labor. Once more, the Supreme Court struck down the law as unconstitutional.

The frustrated reformers next attempted to amend the Constitution in order to ban child labor. Not even the Supreme Court could tamper with a Constitutional amendment. But amending the United States Constitution is a cumbersome process. The child labor amendment failed to receive the ɪɪecessary approval of three quarters of the state legislatures.

Finally, the reformers insisted that all states enforce their school attendance laws. The reformers reasoned that if children were in classrooms they could not be exploited in factories. The tactic was successful. By the 1920s, the wholesale exploitation of child workers began to subside.

In 1938, Congress passed what was called the Fair Labor Standards Act. A provision of the act held that children had to be at least sixteen before they could work full time. Any goods made by children could not be shipped across state lines. It was essentially the same law as the Keating-Owens Act that had been passed some twenty years earlier. This time, a Supreme Court with new members—justices who were not so sympathetic to big business—upheld the law.

The Fair Labor Standards Act marked the end of a century-old stain on American history. Children had begun to be exploited by industry when the first textile mills opened in New England in the early 1800s. The exploitation reached its peak at the turn of the century when masses of immigrants flocked to the country's shores and the factory system

flourished. Finally, after a hundred years, the sad story of child labor in America was over. The provisions of the Fair Labor Standards Act still govern children under the age of sixteen who work after school and on Saturdays.

In only one area does the exploitation of child labor continue on a limited scale. That area is field work on large farms or orchards. Whole families are hired to bring in crops during harvest time. Field workers are often called migrant workers because they migrate from state to state, following the harvests. Because they move so frequently, laws simply cannot catch up with the migrant workers. Even today, young children work long hours in the fields in defiance of the child labor laws. As was true eighty years ago, many of those young field workers are foreign born. Perhaps some day the sickness that is child labor will be truly and forever stamped out in America.

About the Author

R. Conrad Stein was born and grew up in Chicago. He enlisted in the Marine Corps at the age of eighteen and served for three years. He then attended the University of Illinois where he received a bachelor's degree in history. He later studied in Mexico, earning an advanced degree from the University of Guanajuato. Mr. Stein is the author of many other books, articles, and short stories written for young people.

Mr. Stein now lives in Chicago with his wife, Deborah Kent, who is also a writer of books for young readers, and their daughter Janna.

About the Artist

Keith Neely attended the School of the Art Institute of Chicago and received a Bachelor of Fine Arts degree with honors from the Art Center College of Design where he majored in illustration. He has worked as an art director, designer, and illustrator and has taught advertising illustration and advertising design at Biola College in La Mirada, California. Mr. Neely is currently a freelance illustrator whose work has appeared in numerous magazines, books, and advertisements. He lives with his wife and five children in Florida.

24 COLLIER HEIGHTS   SEP 3   1986

Stein, R. Conrad.
    The story of child labor laws / by R.
Conrad Stein ; illustrated by Keith
Neely. -- Chicago : Childrens Press,
1984.
    p. cm. -- (Cornerstones of freedom)
    Summary: Traces the history of laws
that were passed during the early
twentieth century to end the
exploitation of child laborers that had
been widespread since the beginning of
the industrial revolution.
    ISBN 0-516-04679-9
    1. Children--Employment--Law and
legislation--United States--History--
Juvenile literature. I. Neely, Keith,
1943-   ill   . II. Title
III. Series